GW00385554

The Gypsy Poems and Ballads

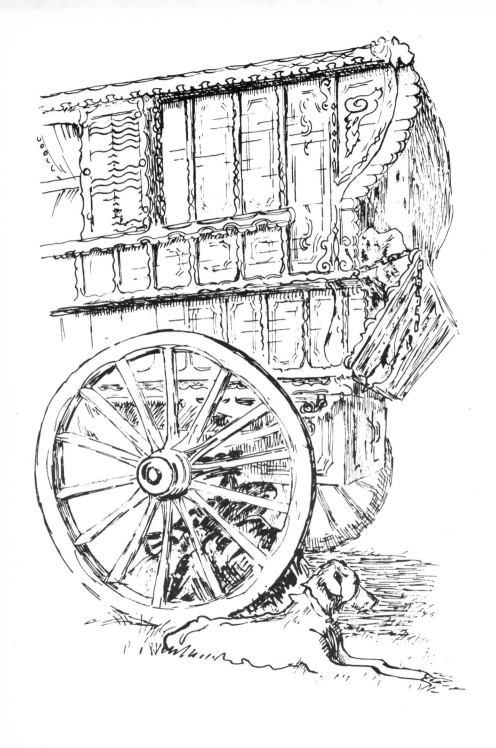

The Gypsy

Poems and Ballads *by Lavengro*

Illustrations by Juliet Jeffery

MIDAS BOOKS

First published in 1973 by
MIDAS BOOKS
12 Dene Way, Speldhurst,
Tunbridge Wells, Kent, TN3 0NX

ISBN 0 85936 015 6

Printed by George Pulman and Sons Ltd
Bletchley, Bucks.

Foreword by Jeremy Sandford

As a young girl living in a Sussex village, Juliet Jeffery became aware of the gypsy caravans which now and again passed along the roads nearby; and became curious about their occupiers. As her painting activities were coming to occupy an ever larger amount of space in her parents' small cottage, she decided it would be a good idea to buy a gypsy caravan to use as a studio. However, she found that she'd become involved in much more than just buying a caravan, for the man she bought it from told her about Appleby — the great annual gypsy meeting place in Westmorland — and Juliet conceived a violent desire to go there.

She achieved her ambition the following year and was fascinated by the complexity and activity of the thousands of gypsies. She wanted to draw them — but at that time was too shy to ask. It was not until her third annual visit that she finally plucked up courage and was delighted to be given permission to draw by every gypsy she asked. It was on this occasion that she first met 'Lavengro'. The poet was eating a breakfast of eggs and bacon, sitting at a low-loader as if it was a table. And they became friends. Two more years passed however before Juliet learned that 'Lavengro' wrote poetry. When she came to read his poems she felt that they expressed, perhaps more than anything else she'd ever read, the things that she was beginning to find valuable in the gypsy culture. She felt that it was important that they should be published and what is more that they should not be 'tidied up' but printed just as he had written them.

The drawings illustrating his work were all done 'from the life', and nearly all at Appleby. She also did various portraits of 'Lavengro' and one of these appears on the cover and another on page 19.

Friendships with other gypsies followed and Juliet now says of Appleby 'I've been there so often that I think the gypsies have come to accept me and my sketch book as part of the scenery.'

'I know that many people these days think of gypsies only as "those terrible people who leave all that rubbish". But to me the rubbish gypsies sometimes leave is nothing like as unpleasant as the incredible ugliness of some housing estates and factories. And I certainly prefer the appearance of the scrap which gypsies deal in to the ugliness of cars in their as yet unscrapped state.

'I prefer to think of the positive side of gypsy culture; I have come to admire, above all, the resilience of the gypsies — or travellers as they prefer to be called. They are both tough and hardy, a necessity in their way of life. How many householders, I wonder, would be prepared to fetch water on a wintry morning in the way that gypsies have to do?

'I admire their economy, particularly their economy of space and it amazes me that a large family will live in a caravan which would fit into just one room of my parents' cottage; also, the scrap metal trade which gypsies practise is of great value to Britain's economy.

'Travellers possess another quality, which I would like to have but which usually eludes me. They are the owners of time, not its slaves. They have time to sit around the camp fire and talk with friends, time simply to gaze into the flames or up at a passing horse.'

This is a book of truth, portraying the lives, capers, faults and failings of the people of the road, also the wisdom and the romantic philosophy, the hardships and perils of the traveller on the road. Ballads of the living and dead to sing around the fireside. Let this book be an object lesson to all young travelling people in this modern age, hoping they will realise what their parents and grandparents had to go through to accumulate the wealth the sons are now diminishing.

Love to them all,

Lavengro

I LOVE THE SOUND

I love the sound of iron and steel,
And the ring of metal too,
For they have earned me many a meal,
And earned me money too.

I love the sound of rustling rags,
The sound of pots and pans,
So I can put them into bags,
When they are in my hands.

I love the sound of wagon wheels,
And of horses feet,
For joy then in my heart will steal,
And make my day complete.

Now I am just a dealing man.
And love these things so well,
Listen to me if you can.
While my love for them I tell.

CUSTY STEW

He hung the pot on the kettle prop,
Over the blazing fire,
The iron pot did hold a lot,
Of all you could desire.

There is chicken, hare and rabbit,
Pheasant and hedgehog too,
What you want we have it,
In the boiling stew.

There are carrots, peas and turnip,
From off the farmers land,
O don't it make you smack your lips,
To smell a stew so grand.

So in a while it will be done,
And we'll all sit around,
For there's enough for everyone,
That are camping on the ground.

9

THE BALLAD OF LADY R.

Before the age of speed began,
When all the fields were green,
Upon the trotting tracks there ran,
A trotting mare supreme.

Her fame was renowned throughout the land,
Her history travelled far,
So get your glass and lift your hand,
To the grey mare, Lady R.

They called her the Guideless Wonder,
That raced on the Raikes Hill track,
Who ran round the track like thunder,
With no driver at her back.

She needed no man nor reins to guide her,
Her sulky wheels were proud,
With the honour that they shared,
Before the cheering crowd.

THE MONEY SPINNER

I bought a horse at Brough Hill Fair,
They said would run away,
I told them that I did not care,
I would drive it home today.

I sold it to a ragbone man,
Who yoked it in his cart,
But once again away it ran,
And so they came to part.

I bought it back for thirty pounds,
Then sold the mare again,
And when the man was on his round,
Again it did the same.

Twenty times I sold that mare,
With great financial gain,
Until an old man knackered her,
And stopped my little game.

THE WHITEGATE BATTLE

Jim Day came down from London Town,
To Blackpool by the sea,
Where Jim Banks had just settled down,
To live so happily.

Now both of them were dealing men,
And rivals of renown,
And there was always trouble,
When together they were found.

Then a farmer had a horse to sell.
And sent for old Jim Day,
But he had told Jim Banks as well,
Upon that very day.

Now on the Whitegate drive they met,
Both driving at great speed,
Each determined not to let,
The other take the lead.

At last the whalebone whips came out,
And battle did begin,
As both of them set about,
To flog the other Jim.

The two gigs raced on side by side,
The horses running wild,
And for one mile down the Whitegate Drive,
The clear air was defiled.

They bumped and bored and slashed and butt,
For near upon a mile,
Until at last they both gave up,
And both began to smile.

So into the farmer's place,
Two gigs drove side by side,
And both agreed that in this case,
The profit they'd divide.

13

BRUSH WAGON

As I went up North, I saw old West,
I saw him following on;
Then my eyes came down to rest,
On a brand new Brush Wagon.

It was being pulled by a big grey mare,
As big as a passing cloud,
And on the front was driving her,
Old Grypher West so proud.

I shouted to my pal Grypher,
'Do you not think that I am blunt,
But why are you driving there
With your wagon back to front?'

'That is the way the wagon was made,'
Old Grypher called to me,
'So just pull up into the shade
And we will make a pot of tea.'

GRANNY'S PIPE

My granny had a little pipe,
And it was made of clay,
It was a thing that she did like,
She smoked it all the day.

She smoked while she made her pegs,
And while she brewed the tea,
She only got upon her legs,
To fill it up you see.

Her daughter and her son,
When they came home each day,
Fetched tobacco by the ton,
So that she could puff away.

And now the pipe is broken,
As granny's gone to rest,
But the pieces are a token,
Of the one we loved the best.

BOOZE UP

From Sedbergh to Kirby,
From there to old Brough Hill,
We'll go into a public house,
Where we'll drink our fill.

We'll fill our bellies up with ale,
With porter and with stout, and
Then we'll fight and bawl and shout,
If they try to kick us out.

We'll sing and dance and fight and trade,
To pass the time away,
At the fair we'll buy the horses up,
At the end of the day.

THE RUINED FAIR

There's a prison camp on Gallows Hill,
Where we are all held inside,
And as it is the Council's will,
We will have to all abide.

They did it all at great expense,
To drive us off the road.
Put us behind a wire fence,
And said that's your new abode.

They put some gravel roads around,
And toilets there as well,
But that is not the camping ground
That we all know so well.

The police they guard us day and night,
Our lives are not our own,
For we do think we have the right
To wander and to roam.

BIRTH OF BLACKPOOL

They came across the water,
Our country side to roam,
And brought their sons and daughters,
To make this land their home.

On the sandhills here they settled,
Behind the old Star Inn,
In wagons bright and speckled,
They brought their kith and kin.

They were Smiths and Lees and Boswells,
All Romanies by birth,
And by their presence you could tell,
They were born to roam the earth.

They were the first attraction,
Which brought people to our shore,
And after them came action,
And our town grew more and more.

Then too the entertainment came,
In every shape and form,
To gain great fame was then the aim,
As Blackpool town was born.

Now she stands out above them all,
The queen of gaiety,
Beneath her tower strong and tall,
The home of variety.

Now the Layton cemetery,
Another Queen does lay,
A gipsy Queen called Boswell,
Who put Blackpool on its way.

17

GYPSY SCHOLAR

A gypsy lad sat by the fire,
His head bent deep in thought,
For he had a great desire,
Better things to be taught.

He wanted to be a scholar
To learn to write and read
With a profession for to follow,
So he would never be in need.

Then he would be the spokesman
For his ancient tribe,
And ignorance would be broke,
As they relied on him with pride.

Now the gypsy boy's dream came true
He passed a high degree.
Now his gypsy family never rue,
That they let him go, you see.

BIRTH PLACE

Every place in England,
I've wandered and I've roamed,
And there's not a place in England,
That I cannot call my home.

I've wandered through all England,
And other countries too,
There's a place in old England,
I always come back to.

It's the little spot in England,
Where my mother gave me birth,
So this little spot in England,
Is the sweetest spot on earth.

And when my wanderings cease on earth,
I will return again,
To the little township of my birth,
And always there remain.

RADGY

They think I am a dinilo,
As radgy as a brush they said.
Yet I made a fortune you know,
Out of iron, brass and lead.

I never had no choro,
Neither any mace,
And wherever I may go,
All men I can face.

Some say I am a kushto mush,
Some say I am a maig,
But with the law I am flush,
So I am not afraid.

For I can buy and sell all them
As radgy as I may be,
To show those little dealing men
Not to make a fool of me.

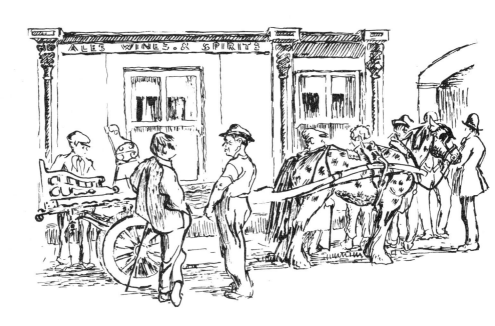

BALLAD OF BUCK BUXTON

It was down in old Lancaster,
In a place called Dalton Square,
Where a brilliant Indian Doctor,
Committed murder there.

He was liked and loved by all,
This man of Indian Birth,
And even now the poor recall,
This kindly Doctor's worth.

But his wife had been unfaithful,
While he attended to the sick,
And to him her name was hateful,
Through this low-down dirty trick.

So one day he did kill,
And dismembered her,
But he left some blood,
Upon the hallway stair.

Now her maid became suspicious,
Of what had happened there,
And the Doctor became vicious,
And had to murder her.

Provocation could have been his plea,
For murdering his wife,
But he had murdered two you see,
And that had cost his life.

Now all the poor in Lancaster,
Mourned on the day he died,
That kindly Indian Doctor,
On who they all relied.

THE TRAIL

They come from the wild Welsh mountains,
To the town of Appleby,
They all come by the leafy lanes,
That ancient fair to see.

They come down from the Scottish glens,
And across the Irish sea,
As everybody recommends,
The fair at Appleby.

They come from cities and from towns,
East, North, South, and West,
Across the moorlands and the downs,
To the fair they like the best.

So please leave room,
On the roads everywhere,
They all go in June,
To the Appleby fair.

COUNTRY FAIR

The Wurlitzer was blaring,
It's music through the air,
And the village folk were sharing
The fun of all the fair.

The wooden horses flew around,
Rearing in the air,
And happiness unbound was found,
Down at the country fair.

The little children they did scream,
With joy and ecstasy,
While all among this pretty scene,
My true love walked with me.

Then in the late hours of the night,
Silence reigned once more.
As they turned out every light,
For the country fair was o'er.

I NEVER STOLE A THING

I swear I never took an hare
Off the farmer's land,
He came out of the gate there
And jumped into my hand.

I never chase a rabbit,
When a keeper is about,
For it is the rabbits' habit,
To follow my old dog out.

Sometimes a farmer's duck or hen,
Will stray right off his land,
Then I will have to rescue them,
I hope you understand.

I never can abide to see,
A game bird in a tree,
I would sooner have its company,
On the table for my tea.

I never put my horses
Among the cows and sheep,
It must have been the fairies
When we were all asleep.

I never touch the farmer's crops
Growing in the ground,
It just jumps into the pot
When I am not around.

The farmer's cows come round at night,
And say 'Please have some milk,
And fill your cans and buckets tight,
With milk as smooth as silk.'

I never take a farmer's gate,
His railing or his trees,
Yet they land upon my fire, mate,
Upon each evening breeze.

I read the farmer's daughter's hand,
And said her crops would grow,
But there was nothing on the land,
By the time I had to go.

NEW SHOES

The ring of the smithy anvil,
Rang down the village street,
While the blacksmith toiled with a will,
Amidst the smithy heat.

An old horse he was standing there,
His hooves all neat and trim,
While the blacksmith did prepare,
A set of shoes for him.

At last the shoes were all complete,
With rubber pads as well,
And placed upon the horse's feet,
And nailed around the shell.

The old horse went out through the door,
And trotted down the road,
For he was feeling young once more,
And fit for any load.

ALL AT THE FAIR

I remember my Romany brothers,
Were all up there at the fair,
Camping there with some others,
On the day I went up there.

They said the fair had been busy
And they had had plenty of trade,
Some of the men had got dizzy
With all the money they made.

They had dealt with horses and harness,
With wagons, tents and carts,
There had been plenty of business
To brighten up all their hearts.

Then they all went to the village,
To celebrate their lucky day,
I knew there was sure to be a rage
So I quietly went on my way.

BATTLING BOWMAN

They called him John Wilf Bowman,
He came from Penrith town.
They said he was a showman,
The way he knocked them down.

He was a quiet and sober man
Until someone did a wrong,
Then away the culprits ran,
As John Wilf came along.

His thundering voice was hard as nails,
His fighting power was supreme,
A terror to the British Isles
Wilf Bowman once had been.

Now like us all, he's getting old,
His fighting days have gone;
Yet we listen to the stories told,
Of Wilfred's carryings on.

26

THE GYPSY AND THE JEW

The gypsy and the Hebrew,
Together were exiled,
From their country that they knew,
Their characters defiled.

As both of them had a part,
In that scene so long ago,
When a man dear to our heart,
Was sacrificed you know.

It was then the men of wealth and power,
Exiled them from their land,
Why, up to this very hour
The world cannot understand.

Now from that day in Bethlehem,
The earth has been their home,
The Hebrew and the gypsy man
Are both destined to roam.

THE GEORDIE BOYS

In County Durham I have friends by the score,
Now in the summertime I will meet them once more,
They will come to the fair in their pony carts,
All to be merry with joy in their hearts.

From Stockton, Durham and Chester-le-Street,
We will hear the patter of their ponies' feet.
From Easington, Hartlepool and Newcastle-on-Tyne,
Every day you see them coming, all the time.

You can always tell when the Geordies arrive
By the shouting and bawling as on the fair they drive.
'How are you my hinny?' is the first thing they will say,
'Have you a pony you want to give away?'

Then back to the land of the Tyne and the Tees,
The Geordies will go in their twos and their threes,
Then we'll say goodbye to them all, as they go,
The boys from the County Durham we know.

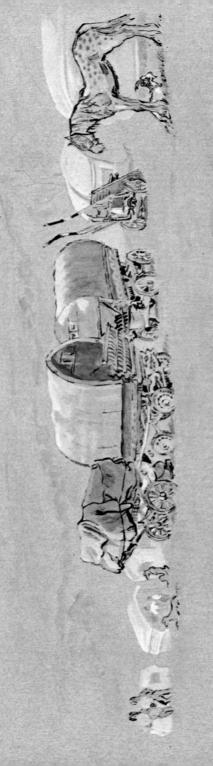

THOSE LOWTHER LASSES

Lowther is a northern name,
That's been there quite a while,
A castle which is called the same,
Stands up there in style.

There are Lowthers in the humble homes,
Also in that castle, fine,
And there's Lowthers who like to roam,
These are the friends of mine.

Their women are like battleships,
They are so big and strong,
They're fifty six around the hips
And nearly six foot long.

Now any man that marries one,
Has to be very brave,
As he will find his freedom gone,
And that he is a slave.

DAD'S WHIP

Our Father's whip hangs on the wall,
Clean and shining bright,
A reminder to us all,
What dear old Dad was like.

A thousand horses had felt its lash,
And some of us had too,
For at a word the whip would flash,
To cut you right in two.

The whip was made of whalebone,
With engraved silver bands,
It was a weapon on its own,
While in a dealers hands.

But now it hangs there on the wall,
While Father's in his grave,
And as we see it we recall,
The service that it gave.

31

CURLY HEADED LITTLE GYPSY

A lady was told by a gypsy one day
Her fortune and future in store,
But the gypsy had gone, sorry to say,
And she hadn't seen her anymore.

Now an old maid, she sits lonely and sad
Her poor heart full of concern,
As she hums a tune that had been
Her prayer for the gypsy's return.

Chorus
Curly headed little gypsy,
When will you come my way?
With your smiling face,
And the beauty of your race,
I'll bless that day.
Come tell me my future, sell me your wares,
Play on your fiddle, romantic airs.
Child of traditional romance,
Memory of a bygone day,
You are the only chance,
I have to make my heart feel gay.
Your life is spent in roaming,
What better could there be,
But you set my heart a-yearning
For your face again to see.

But at night they appeared in a dream,
The gypsies of the village green,
And as if in answer to her prayer,
She woke to find the gypsy there.

THE FADING WAGON

The paint on the wagon was faded,
The gold lines and scrolls were all dull,
Its owner was now getting staid,
For his life had been lengthy and full.

The hoops on the wagon were rusty,
The springs and the shackles were bare.
It was a pity to see a wagon so trusty,
Was sadly in need of repair.

The cover was just like its owner,
Old with the passing of time,
Both led the life of a roamer,
In peaceful surroundings divine.

But the owner can never afford now,
To make his old wagon like new,
So he'll just have to manage somehow,
That's all the poor fellow can do.

APPLEBY TRAIL

They come from the South, the East and the West,
And from the North, to the Fair they like best.
They will all be coming soon,
Setting the trail on the first of June.

They'll be bringing their horses, wagons and carts,
Choosing their courses with joy in their hearts.
They will wet their whistle every now and then,
And have a bit of a crack with dealing men.

They will stop each night in a different place,
Slowly going on, never in a haste
Chopping and changing when they rest
Each one trying to get tackle of the best.

Then they will all bear down
On every road around
To occupy old Appleby town
And the camping ground.

They come from the South, the East and the West,
And from the North, to the Fair they like best.
They will all be coming soon,
Setting the trail on the first of June.

GLOWING FIRES

I will be there when the camp-fires glow,
I will be there just in time you know.
I'm setting off now, I'm half way up the row,
To there where the camp fires glow.

Up there where the camp-fires glow,
Just save a place for me,
As I am coming on slow
There is no telling how long I'll be.

So please keep the fires alive,
Let the grey smoke rise high in the sky,
Until the time I arrive,
Up in those hills so high.

So please save me a place on the hillside,
There midst the fires so bright
So I too can watch all the smoke rise,
Keeping warm well into the night.

THE OLD DAYS

Sitting around the camp-fire,
Drinking from a jar,
Couldn't rouse a donkey,
Never mind a motor car.

Cannot afford a drink,
Cannot raise a yoke.
Whatever can a man do, when
He's gone and lost his poke?

I'll have to get a bran sack,
And wander down the road,
Calling at the back streets,
Until I get a load.

Even if it's raining,
Even if it's fine,
I'll have to feed those
Little kids of mine.

39

WOLF TOOTH BALLAD

I walked into a stable, about a mile away,
And saw a horse unable to eat its corn or hay.
' I'll sell it for a knacker,' the owner said to me,
Then I looked in its mouth and found it was only three.

I put upon its barren frame
A woollen horses sheet,
Then I walked it home again,
Quietly through the street.

I held its head up in the air,
When I did get inside,
And with the wolf tooth I saw there,
No horse could survive.

I got my hammer and chisel then,
And chopped that wolf-tooth out.
I did it in my little den,
When no-one was about.

I then made him a nice warm feed,
Or bran and linseed oil;
Which he golluped down with greed,
Until his blood did boil.

Day by day he ate and ate,
I slowly watched him grow,
And thought what would have been his fate,
By one that did not know.

But now he is quite fit again,
And still has two broad teeth,
For beneath the barren frame
A big red heart did beat.

SMOKEY DOG

The old dog was tired,
As beneath the wagon he lay,
Smokey had retired,
As he had seen his day.

No more would he chase the hares around,
For his eyes were growing dim,
He stayed around the camping ground,
That was the place for him.

He still was proud and faithful,
His scars showed that he'd been,
With children he was playful,
While playing on the green.

Now he was to guard the ground,
When everyone is out,
But nobody will come around,
While Smokey is about.

GONE ARE THE DAYS

Gone are the days at Appleby fair,
When there were only horses up there,
Gone are the wagons with covers of green,
And no longer can camp fires be seen.

There were the Parkers, Lamberts and Wrights,
Whose rattles disturbed the peace of the nights,
Gone are the plaids and the silks on the men,
Gone is the gaiety that we had then.

Singing and fighting went on the time,
And hundreds of horses were tied in a line.
Now that's all over, things aren't the same,
And never will never come back again.

COMING HOME

From the Fellend to the Brackens,
Our horses knees do bend.
And the whalebone whips are cracking,
Until Kirkby Bank does end.

From the Brackens down to Devil's Bridge,
The wagons roll along,
Up the hills and o'er the ridge,
On the road we've known so long.

Cart and accommodation,
Trailers by the score,
Full of our relations,
That we have met once more.

Then on to Clapham Common,
Or in to Melling Lane
We will say farewell to someone,
As we wander home again.

For now the fair is over,
Until another year,
And though some might be in clover,
Some could shed a tear.

MOVE ON

Move on, move on, said the old policeman,
To the gypsies by the road,
Move on, move on, to where you can,
And find some new abode.

You cannot stay here where you are,
Upon the Queen's highway,
You have to make room for the motorcar,
For the horse has had its day.

Your iron tyres cut up the road,
Your speed it is too slow,
So gather up your little load,
Then away you go.

Move on, move on, is all they say,
What can a gypsy do,
But move on until his dying day,
To find some pastures new.

LITTLE SCOTTISH WAGON

I have owned a Yorkshire wagon,
And a London wagon too,
But a little Falkirk wagon,
Is big enough for two.

I'm going to take a little bride,
Away from her mothers home,
Then together we will ride,
On all the roads we roam.

We will deal and hawk our way along,
Through all the countryside,
And whether things go right or wrong,
We'll still be side by side.

Then some day I will buy,
A car and trailer grand,
And pass my Falkirk wagon by,
And quickly wave my hand.

47

MOTHER PREPARED

My mother's face was wrinkled,
Her hands were brown and gnarled,
Yet her old eyes twinkled,
As her life she recalled.

Twenty years she had roamed about,
Since her childhood days,
And she could tell you all about,
The travelling people's ways.

She told us how she met our Dad,
Upon the Queen's highway,
When he was just a strapping lad,
And she was young and gay.

Each recollection brings a smile,
On to her wrinkled face,
Although she knows that in a while,
She'll reach her resting place.

PAINT BRUSH GENIUS

My Uncle Abraham,
Whose hearing was hard,
Up to me ran,
In the Auction yard.

'I am wanting a wagon,'
He said to me,
'As mine has just gone,
And homeless I be.'

Now I have the wagon,
Back at my home,
And that is the one,
That you're going to own.

One wheel wants hooping,
The paintwork is bare,
It wants touching up
I do declare.

But you are the master,
With a brush in the hand,
And I know the wagon,
It will come out grand.

Abraham bought the wagon,
And started with glee
For none put the paint on
Like old Abraham Lee.

When his painting was done,
The folk gathered round,
As it shone like the sun,
On the old camping ground.

THE GYPSY WARNING

'You have a good and kindly face,'
Said the gypsy at the door,
'So if a coin in my hand you place,
I will tell you more,'

I put a coin into her hand,
To see what she would say,
And she said I'd see a foreign land,
Many miles away.

She said I'd meet a dark hansome man,
With a kind and loving way,
Which would alter every plan.
That I had made that day.

Now what she said has all come true,
Which I do now regret,
As now I've a fatherless baby to
The young man that I met.

MOTHER'S GOLDEN PIECE

My mother wore a five pound piece,
Hung on a golden chain,
And now my sister has that piece,
It is where it will remain.

The piece it is a Jubilee,
Of Queen Victoria's reign,
And though it don't belong to me,
I like it just the same.

For now it has great value,
It is thirty times it's price,
And just between you and me,
I think that's very nice.

But now just for our mother's sake,
That piece would not be sold,
However much that it would make,
We will keep that piece of gold.

50

PLAYBOY'S BRIDE

He bought her a brand new trailer,
And a powerful motor car.
He gave her silver and bought her gold,
He got her china — rare and old.

He dressed her in silks and satins,
And put a rose in her hair,
And put a ring on her finger —
A ring beyond compare.

Then after a while he left her
Alone, in the trailer at nights,
While he went out with the boys
To see the brighter lights.

She rued the day she'd married
And became a playboy's wife,
And she longed to be back with her people,
To lead their simple life.

Then came to her door a poor boy,
Whom she had liked long ago,
So she gave up her wealth and riches
And went with him in the snow.

She left behind her silver,
She left behind her gold,
She took off her silks and satins,
And put on her clothes of old.

Now she goes out with her basket
Like her mother used to do,
And at night she sits by the camp-fire,
With her young man good and true.

53

MY OWN HOME

A golden ray of sunshine,
Shone upon the wagon top,
For it is that home of mine,
This little open lot.

It had been newly painted,
It's sheet was new and green,
Nowhere was it tainted,
It's inside bright and clean.

It's little stove was shining chrome,
There was carpet on the floor,
And for a man this lot to own,
What could he wish for more?

Now I am looking for a wife,
My children for to bear,
And to lead a happy life,
In this wagon just with her.

JULIA AND OLIVER

Julia and Oliver,
Bought a cottage by the sea,
And Julia said to Oliver,
'This is no place for me.

The green grass it is growing,
The sun does shine once more,
And now it's Spring I'm going
Around the country I adore.

I hear the little birdies sing,
I see the flowers in bloom,
I cannot stand this brick built thing,
I will have to leave it soon.

So get the horses from the field,
And pull the wagon out,
And make the cottage doors sealed
While no-one is about.'

54

THE FIGHTING COCK

He was only a battered fighting cock,
Who had fought for many a year,
Of his many fights he'd won a lot,
Now his end was drawing near,

His feathers were all tattered,
His neck was red and sore,
To him it never mattered,
If he never fought no more.

He once had been the pride and joy,
Of every fighting pit,
And hundreds came to enjoy,
And see him fighting fit.

Now his only eye is closing,
His comb is hanging low,
But still his memory will last,
Where fighting cocks do go.

DODGY GRY

To Hell, to Hell, with that old Boswell,
He sold me a dodgy gry,
For he knew well he could tell,
That I would never cry.

He said it was as sound as a bell,
And could pull any load,
Now I will flog that old Boswell,
If I see him down the road.

For he knew I had a young family,
So a good gry I had to have,
But he sold that one to me,
And I think he is too bad.

Now he forgets in days gone by,
When he had troubles too,
So why did the old dog try,
And say that gry was true?

LINO BOYS

Just raise your hats to the lino boys,
Who stand in the market place,
On a box in an easy poise,
With a smile upon their face.

They will sell you a roll at half the price,
Or just a yard or two,
And tell you that it's very nice,
And just the thing for you.

They will stretch it out from here to there,
And say there's quite a lot,
And guarantee that you will declare,
What a bargain you have got.

They say that they have treated you right,
And send you on your way,
Then they prepare for a merry night,
With the money you did pay.

LEE GAP

The Bradford boys were battling,
At the Lee Gap fair.
One of them was challenging,
To fight all that were there.

A little man stepped from a tent,
And shouted 'There you are,
Will you tell me what you meant,
You there with the scar?'

'I said I would fight anyone!'
The Bradford boy declared,
'Alright man, I will take you on,
So get yourself prepared.'

The tent man carved the Bradford,
With hands made of cement,
Until the Bradford boys all ran,
And he went back to his tent.

THE BLUE RIBBON

It was the Epsom Derby day,
The blue ribbon of the turf,
And you hear all the people say
It's the greatest race on earth.

The horses are of high degree,
The finest in the land,
And all of noble pedigree,
That's what we understand.

Truly one cannot forget,
The crowds are so immense
Who go to have a look and bet,
With nerves and muscles tense.

The crowds all stand up and roar,
As the horses reach the post,
For they have been to see once more,
The race they love the most.

It was Epsom Derby day,
The blue ribbon of the turf,
And you hear all the people say,
It's the greatest race on earth.

THE OLD FAT HEN

A big fat hen was boiling,
In a pan above the fire,
While a gypsy man was toiling,
With a broken wagon tyre.

The lurcher dog was lying,
Beside the wagon wheel,
The children they were playing,
Waiting for their meal.

The mother was out hawking,
To earn their daily bread,
The son was out there talking,
To a farmer in a shed.

Soon they'd all sit down together,
When the big fat hen was done,
And the old peg knife would sever,
A piece for everyone.

RUN AWAY

I yoked a pony in my cart,
That I bought yesterday,
It gave a buck and then a start,
And tried to run away.

The reins, they would not hold it,
It's mouth was much too hard.
It got a firm grip on the bit,
And ran out of the yard.

We galloped down the highway,
While people looked in fright,
As I pulled and tugged away,
At the reins with all my might.

Then just as I was giving up,
Before I woke up dead,
Two brawny lads came rushing up,
And grabbed the pony's head.

TRACK TRAGEDY

The sulky wheels were rotting,
As they hung down from the roof,
While below on the wall was hanging,
A mounted pony's hoof.

They were a sad reminder,
Of an awful tragedy,
And we would think it kinder,
If they were not there to see.

While racing round a track one day,
Approaching record time,
A sulky wheel had given way,
When all was going fine.

The sulky jammed into the ground,
Both horse and driver fell,
And both were dead when they were found,
That pair we loved so well.

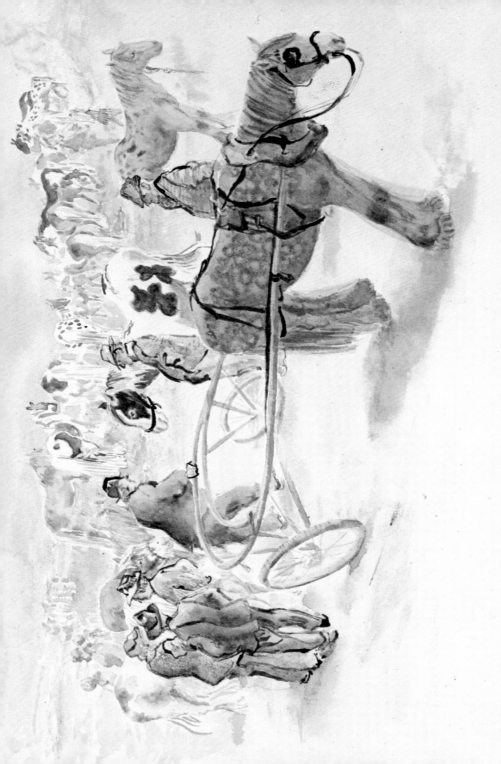

THE STRANGER

Each year an old man comes around,
And stays against our home,
He stays upon some open ground,
Where he is all alone.

He must be a gypsy man,
For he lives in a tent,
He comes and goes where'er he can,
And never pays rent.

He knows not of income tax,
He does no work at all,
He only walks the country tracks,
This old man straight and tall.

What he has been throughout his life,
He never will disclose,
Or if he ever had a wife,
It is only him that knows.

CHILDHOOD TRAVEL

It's the roads on which I travelled,
That I am going on again,
Where my memory will unravel,
And take me back again.

To when our family was united
And travelled in a line,
When the children got excited,
For everything was fine.

The wagons kept on rolling along,
The horses tied behind,
A lovely sight to gaze upon,
One to stay in your mind.

I know that scene cannot come back,
In the same way as before,
Yet still I'll follow down the track,
And think of it once more.

CAGED BIRD

They took away his freedom,
And his liberty,
When to prison he had gone,
For fighting don't you see.

They put him in a prison cell,
Like a tiger in a cage,
Which did anger him you could tell,
And filled his heart with rage.

He paced about the narrow space,
A captive of mankind,
The loneman of the gypsy race
No freedom there could find.

So now for months will he be there,
Away from kith and kin,
And on release he will declare,
No more will they get him.

GYPSY MUSIC MAN

I am the gypsy music man,
That plays there at the fair,
I play all the tunes I can,
Both old and new and rare.

I play the tunes my father knew,
And modern pop as well,
When all the notes I play ring true,
Just like a chiming bell.

Now if you want some opera tunes,
Or a melody from a show,
To ask me, do not be afraid,
For I'll play it through you know.

So when you do go to the fair,
Just listen for a while,
To the music I play there
In my old familiar style.

RABBIT AND SCOLLOPS

Old Gaskin was building a wagon,
When his old peg knife broke,
As he had many carvings to carve on,
He didn't think it a joke.

He then took his wood to the wheelwright,
And said 'Will you do something for me?'
The wheelwright said 'Yes, John alright,
If you catch me a rabbit for tea.'

So John sent his old dog out hunting,
While he smoked his old pipe on a stile,
And the old dog kept coming back panting,
Placing rabbits in a pile.

So old John could finish his wagon,
And the wheelwright have rabbit for tea,
And now the betting is ten to one,
That wagon is at old Appleby.

COUSIN OF MINE

Cousin of mine,
Where are you all this time?
I try to follow each road you go,
But never can catch you, you know.

I look for the signs,
And the tracks of your wheels,
And if you've left behind,
An horse in a field.

I ask in each village and each little town,
But alas! cousin, I can't track you down.
All that I ask cannot tell me the way,
On which you have travelled today.

So, little cousin, just wait for a while,
There, in a shady old lane,
Until I come there, driving in style,
Just to be with you again.

GYPSY SAMARITAN

One night out there in the snow,
I heard music sweet and low,
It was an old man playing a piccolo,
With nowhere to go.

I asked him into my wagon
To warm himself at my stove,
As he had very few clothes on,
He might have easily froze.

He told me all about himself,
And what he had been through,
As he always had bad health,
So little could he do.

I told him to sleep in my spare tent,
And I would feed him every day,
And now he could rest content,
Until the snow all went away.

EMPTY LINE

Old Sack Finney was fishing,
Down by a babbling brook,
Old Sack there was wishing,
He could catch a fish to cook.

All of a sudden his old rod bent,
And old Sack gave a hoot,
It wasn't the fish he thought it meant,
It was only an old tramp's boot.

He threw it back into the brook,
Uttering an awful word,
The fishes all came up to look,
At the swear word they had heard.

Then the fishes turned against old Sack,
And would not bite his hook,
So old Sack then had to go back,
Without a fish to cook.

HENRY'S MODEL 'T'

In all America's history,
No finer sight was seen,
Than Henry's little model 'T',
When he pulled it on the green.

He had to knock down half his home,
To get his motor out,
For he built it inside alone,
When no one was about.

A revelation to all mankind,
Was this on what they gazed,
Which left all previous things behind,
And had the world amazed.

Here was the poor man's friend at last,
For ever for to be,
For the motor's future then was cast,
In Henry's model 'T'.

It had no gears to go wrong,
No batteries to go flat,
Its body it was light, neat and strong,
And as nimble as a cat.

A million models there was sold,
In all the world around,
Its value it was that of gold,
Where ever it was found.

A hundred pounds, it was the price,
From 1917,
A great demand it did suffice,
It was the poor man's dream.

May Henry's body rest in peace,
Wherever it may be,
For he did give the world at least,
His famous model 'T'.

GOOD LUCK BROTHERS

Our cousins and our brothers,
Are scattered o'er the earth,
Where their fathers and their mothers,
Are Romanies by birth.

We all have the same mode of life,
And a language of our own,
And each has got a gypsy wife,
To run his little home.

Each year we have a meeting place,
Where we can all unite
To hear the news of all our race,
Their fortunes and their plight.

Then we all go upon our way,
To find some pastures new,
And to our brothers we will say,
May Good Luck go with you.

GRAVES OF MEMORIES

As I walked in the cemetery,
Round the graves of travelling men,
It brought back a memory,
Of the days I spent with them.

I saw the graves of young men,
Who died within their prime,
And I knew that all of them,
Had once been friends of mine.

I also saw the graves of those,
Who harder times had seen,
Who I had seen upon the road,
And stayed with on the green.

Yet soon I will be there with them,
Deep down below the road,
On which do roam travelling men,
Men of no fixed abode.

NO CAMPING

Everywhere in England
No camping can be seen
For they're locking up itinerants
For camping on the green.

They cannot graze their horses
Or break their motorcars,
Throw away their tincans,
Bottles, or their jars.

And if there are no toilets
For many miles around,
They are locking up itinerants
For messing up the ground.

Very soon we will all be found
Behind a high wire fence
In some city camping ground
To live at great expense.

THE THREE NAILS

Where is that man Jesus?
Have you seen him on the road?
Or is he still forsaking us,
By giving us no abode?

He left us to roam the earth,
Without our own country,
Wandering as we are from birth
Over land and sea.

We had saved his life for him,
On the cross at Calvary,
When four nails were made for him,
But they got only three.

The gypsies had made them nails,
And stole one for themselves,
So you can thank the gypsy men
That he now in heaven dwells.

Where is that man Jesus?
Have you seen him on the road?
Or is he still forsaking us,
By giving us no abode?

THE LORD GIVETH

The Lord he gave the Heaven,
To the sun and moon and stars,
But he gave the land to the travelling man,
To wander near and far.

He gave the rivers and the streams
The bylanes and the dunes
Just to fill the traveller's dream
That he could settle soon.

He gave the meadows of green grass,
So their animals could graze,
And they could settle there at last,
Their families for to raise.

But now the world has run amok,
With turmoil all around,
And the travelling man has had his lot,
Stuck in a camping ground.

MODERN ITINERANTS

You can have your Mercedes Benz,
You can have your Jaguar and Rolls,
But I will have a Dales bred mare,
And lots of little foals.

You can have your Eccles trailers,
Your Berkleys and Lunedales,
But I've my bow topped wagon,
To take me down to Wales.

You can have your Cromby coats,
Your silk shirts and your suits,
But I will wear old plaid shirts,
Silks and Luton boots.

You talk of Grands for motorcars,
As easy as can be,
But a hundred horses had your Dad,
For that price you must see.

THE TINKER'S DAUGHTERS

Down by the Derwent Waters,
We camped not long ago,
With a tinker and his daughters,
Who were very nice to know.

At night we all went dancing,
In a village by the lake,
All the time romancing,
Just for old times sake.

Now of the tinker's daughters,
We fell in love with two,
Down by the Derwent Waters,
Me and my brother too.

So we married the tinker's daughters,
And live in harmony,
Down by the Derwent Waters
Where we chose our destiny.

78

BILL WRIGHT'S

A fine thing of beauty it was in its day,
And made at the village of old Rothwell heigh.
Good luck to Bill Wright and his wagons fine,
They were the best of them all in their time.

The brass-ended naves and big highset wheels,
Were ideal for taking you over the fields.
Folk they all stared at it, when on the road,
For it ran on like velvet while carrying a load.

Good luck to Bill Wright for his carving supreme,
And for making a wagon that's a traveller's dream.

WRIGHT'S WAGON

A Bill Wright's Wagon stood on the road,
Its bows swelled out with pride,
That it was King of all the road,
No one had yet denied.

Just look at its high wheels behind,
With naves of solid brass,
And its carving you will find,
Will be hard to surpass.

Look at its big cradle lock,
Built so neat and strong,
Watch it turn and sway and rock,
As it goes along.

Look at its pan box behind,
With amber handles on,
And the rack above as you will find
Has room for anyone.

It's inside is as perfect,
As anyone could wish,
You can never find a defect,
In a wagon built like this.

It runs along like velvet,
And it's pulled about with ease,
And no man has ever yet,
Built the like of these.

A Bill Wright's Wagon stood on the road,
Its bows swelled out with pride,
That it was King of all the road,
No one had yet denied.

GRY PAL

I have a pal I like the best,
Who is faithful and so true,
And when I put him to the test,
He always pulls me through.

His mane is to his shoulder point,
His tail trails on the floor,
He is sound in every limb and joint,
What man could ask for more?

His bonnie head is small and sweet,
His colour fallow bay,
His leg hair falls upon his feet,
Which are a steely grey.

His chest is broad, his back is stout,
Feet like a mason's mall,
So if you see him rear and snort
You will know that he's my pal.

83

THE KETTLE PROP

The kettle prop lay rusting,
In the long damp grass,
For it had been forsaken,
For the calor gas.

No longer did it proudly stand,
Stuck into the ground,
Holding up a stewpot grand,
While they all sat around.

The fire below did warm it,
And its hook it got so hot,
But now it had been thrown away,
And left there to rot.

The iron kettle and the stewpan,
That he held in the air,
Were thrown out to the ragman,
They were not wanted there.

Then one day some anxious hands,
Came feeling in the grass.
Things had all gone wrong with them,
They had no calor gas.

Now loving hands did close around,
That rusting piece of iron,
And as they stuck it in the ground,
It felt just like a lion.

UNDERNEATH THE VARDO

Underneath the vardo,
The little jukel lay,
Tied up to the bedpiece,
He lay there all the day.

Then when I let him loose once more,
He scampered off so swift and sure,
And brought me back a shoshoi,
Up to my wagon door.

Up came the rai
From the bori kair,
And rokkered in my earhole
'What are you doing there?'

'Oh! my lord and gentle man
Forgive me this time, if you can,
For I am full of sorrow,
Come with me and you'll see.'

I took him in the vardo,
Where my chavies lay,
Crying for their mammy,
That was so far away.

For she had left us long ago,
Where she'd gone we did not know,
Me and my chavies,
My only Gypsy lee.

The rai looked around him,
Then he said to me,
'Man you've had your troubles,
It's very plain to see.

And as you wander on your way,
May luck go with you night and day,
You and your chavies,
Your little Gypsy Lee.'

BUCKA BROW

Up Bucka Brow I got somehow
My horses they were sweating,
As I am not so active now
For older I am getting.

Now at the top I will rest awhile,
And smoke my old clay pipe,
Then down the Brow I'll go in style,
As steady as I like.

Then I have Kirkby Bank to face,
And my wagon weighs a ton,
So up the hill I'll have to race,
To get a decent run.

So now my lads won't I be glad
When I get to the fair,
After the struggle I have had,
To get my wagon there.

BOYS OF THE OLD BRIGADE

Where are the boys of the Old Brigade,
With their plaid shirts and their Luton Boots ?
Where are these boys so bold and brave,
The boys with the dark gypsy looks ?

Where are the handkies they wore all the time,
The Kingsmen, Paisley and Birds Eye so fine
And the special suits they all wore,
And the velvet trousers they adore.

Their Larner and Larner they carried,
All round the country to every little fair,
Where are their wagons and little Bradford carts ?
Where are the women that captured their hearts ?

Hawking round houses and farms,
With little yellow baskets hanging from arms,
Try to remember those old days if you can,
For that was the end of the old travelling man.

HILL CLIMB

A cavalcade of caravans,
Went slowly up the hill,
The rattle of their iron bands,
Rang through the air still.

The horses they were struggling,
The men ran by their side,
All of them were straining,
To reach the other side.

For it had been a long, long pull,
You dare not risk a stop,
But the horses were all powerful,
And slowly reached the top.

Then at the top they stayed the night,
To cook and rest and sleep,
To start off at the morning light,
Their journey to complete.

BARRI TRAILER

Come all my gypsy cousins,
Wherever you may be,
Come down in your dozens,
And see what you can see.

You'll see my brand new trailer,
All cut glass and chrome.
I bought it off a tailor,
Who lived in it alone.

He was going to join his daughter,
Far across the sea,
But he could not cross the water,
In his trailer, don't you see.

Oh! cousins, when you come along,
There will be envy in your heart,
And though you all will bid me strong,
I don't think I will part.

91

SHE BELONGS TO ME

Her mother was a Boswell,
Her father was a Lee,
And now she's changed her name again,
For she belongs to me.

We cannot raise a wagon,
Cannot raise a gry,
We have to always mong a lift
Off gorgios passing by.

Our home it is a willow tan,
Beneath an old hedgerow,
At night we have to cuddle up,
We've nowhere else to go.

We have a lurcher dog, you know,
To fill the shoshoi pot,
So wherever we may go,
We will not want a lot.

Tomorrow we will wander on
As happy as can be,
And if we meet upon the road
I'll tell your future that I see.

GYPSY LAMENT

Where are the roads and lanes where we roamed ?
Where are the commons where we made our homes ?
Where are the roadsides where our horses grazed ?
Where is the beauty on which we once gazed ?

Where are the woods where we gathered herbs ?
What is it that has frightened away the birds ?
Where are the hedgehogs, rabbits, hares ?
Where is the sport in which our dogs shared ?

Where are the trout streams and ponds full of frogs,
Are they like all things — gone to the dogs ?
Where are the people that welcomed us back ?
They have all disappeared leaving no track.

Gone is our freedom, our love and our life,
A pain in the heart to both man and wife;
For there go our hopes and all of our dreams,
All swallowed up in new housing schemes.

SIGNPOST

On the corner stands a post,
That is pointing to my home.
It is the post that I love most,
As I walk the road alone.

No other post or milestone,
Can mean the same to me,
As it shows me my way home,
To my wife and family.

No matter where I go each day,
Or milestones may I pass,
That signpost always seems to say,
You are nearly home at last.

It is my guardian angel,
When I have been to town,
And what I'd do I cannot tell
If they took that signpost down.

THE LAST JOURNEY

The big black hearse moved slowly on,
Away from the wagon door,
While all the people gazed upon
Him they would see no more.

All his fond relations,
And his bosom friends,
Walked behind in meditation,
To see him to his end.

Six hundred travellers followed him,
They came by plane and car.
Each family brought their kith and kin,
From towns and cities far.

Now there's just a memory,
And a granite stone that stands,
Beneath which lies for eternity,
Of him that roamed the lands.

94

MY BOOK

It is the last page in my book
That I have wrote with pride,
So pick it up and have a look,
And see what is inside.

You'll see that I have tried my best
To put my thoughts in words,
And that I'm not just like the rest,
Following the herds.

I like to think I'm different,
With ideas of my own,
And many hours have been spent,
Writing it alone.

Now I hope you will approve of it,
When you have read it through,
And find it full of sense and wit,
And nothing crude and blue.

Afterword by Juliet Jeffery

I would like to thank Lavengro for allowing me to illustrate his works, and both of us would like to thank my father for introducing us in the first place. Furthermore, my father has been a model of patience and kindness on my sketching jaunts.

In addition I would like to thank the travellers who have allowed me to invade their privacy in making these sketches, and I hope they will let me go on doing this.

I should lastly like to thank the Gypsy Lore Society who kindly permitted me to refer to a photograph of the Brush Wagon, taken by the late Mr. Fred Shaw.